My First Acrostic

The East & West Midlands

Edited by Angela Fairbrace

First published in Great Britain in 2010 by:

Young Writers
Remus House
Coltsfoot Drive
Peterborough
PE2 9JX
Telephone: 01733 890066
Website: www.youngwriters.co.uk

All Rights Reserved
© Copyright Contributors 2010
SB ISBN 978-0-85739-137-7

Foreword

The 'My First Acrostic' collection was developed by Young Writers specifically for Key Stage 1 children. The poetic form is simple, fun and gives the young poet a guideline to shape their ideas, yet at the same time leaves room for their imagination and creativity to begin to blossom.

Due to the young age of the entrants we have enjoyed rewarding their effort by including as many of the poems as possible. Our hope is that seeing their work in print will encourage the children to continue writing as they grow and develop their skills into our poets of tomorrow.

Young Writers was established in 1990 to nurture creativity in our children and young adults, to give them an interest in poetry and an outlet to express themselves. This latest collection will act as a milestone for the young poets and one that will be enjoyable to revisit again and again.

Contents

Sophia Field (7) 1

Alvaston Junior Community School, Derby
Denisa Krasniqi (7) 1

Bishopton Primary School, Stratford Upon Avon
Bethany Hayward (6) 2
Reece Stanley (7) 3
Jamie Storey (6) 3
Madeline Macleod (7) 4
Jack Smith (6) 4
Joshua Wasley (6) 5
Amy Harris (7) 6
Emma Dyke (7) 6
Jaaouine Imane (7) 7
Jake Hartnett (7) 7

Bournebrook CE Primary School, Fillongley
Alyssa Jardim (6) 8
Seth Nesbitt (7) 8
Jake James-Preece (7) 9
Daniel Sutton (7) 9
Emma Newcombe (6) 10
Haidee Davies (7) 10
Holly Guise (7) 11
Samuel Billington (6) 11
Rebecca Smith (6) 12
Katelyn Acton (7) 12
Michael Whitehouse (6) 13
Reef Billingham (6) 13
Ella Lawrence (7) 14

Church Vale Primary School, Warsop
Owen Keelan (6) 14
Keaton Ellis (7) 15
Caitlin Payne (7) 15
Tate O'Neill (7) 16
Mazie Piontek (6) 16
Leyah Swinn (7) 17

Eloise O'Donnell (6) 17
Katie Warren (6) 18
Katie Morris (6) 18
Annice Murphy (6) 19
Joey Root (6) 19
Joseph Bramley Bird (6) 20

Coomb Briggs Primary School, Immingham
Mia Montgomery (7) 20
Rhiannon Graves (7) 21
Olivia Black (7) 21
Charlie Bates (6) & Lewis Knox 22
Eloise Owens (7) 22

Frodingham Infant School, Scunthorpe
Ashleigh Barley (7) 23
Teri Pell (6) 23
Reece Fullerton (7) 24
Joshua Brader (7) 24
Tyler Marshall (7) 25
Hannah Jordan (7) 25
George McLean (7) 26
Ellie Mae Holmes (6) 26
Brandon Poole (7) 27
Bethany Patrick (7) 27
Holly Jacklin (7) 28
Jack Parratt Guntrip (6) 28
Ciaran Sykes (7) 29
Kieran Busby (6) 29
Jasmine Calder (6) 30
Wesley Jay Pearce (7) 31
Hannah Whittaker (6) 32
Reece Moir (6) 32
Nathan Ferguson (7) 33
Katie Craven (7) 33
Leah Sweeting (7) 34
Aberam Prathaban (6) 35
Corey Lewis (7) 36
Chloe Grierson (7) 36
Fayaz Badruddoza (6) 37
Kacper Jakimowski (7) 37

Ellie-Mae Jackson (6) ... 38
Dylan Lovell (7) ... 38

Gosberton Community Primary School, Gosberton
Samuel Jackson (6) ... 39
Joseph Cowling (5) ... 39
Maria Woods (6) ... 40
Levi Tolson (6) ... 40
Mellyssa Doades (6) ... 41
Tia Leoni Shirley (5) ... 41
Joe Maltby (5) ... 42
Alexander Stacey (6) ... 42
Ella Everest (6) ... 43

Heathfield School, Kidderminster
Cormac Wolstenholme (6) ... 43
Hannah Baker (6) ... 44
Jack Wharton (6) ... 45
Darcy Scott Worrall (7) ... 46
Sebastian Mitchell (6) ... 46
Joseph Hallowell (6) ... 47
Leah Tidmarsh (6) ... 48
Oliver Bailey (6) ... 49
Lucy Newton (6) ... 50
Evie Tonks (6) ... 51
Molly Mae Hall (5) ... 52
Eve Sinclair-Hall (5) ... 53
Emily Diaz (5) ... 54
Robert Cox (5) ... 54
Brooklyn Taylor (6) ... 55

Huttoft Primary School, Alford
Iona Jones (6) ... 55
Zoe Burton (6) ... 56
Emily Barker (6) ... 56
Jacob Skinner (7) ... 57
Michelle Virgo (7) ... 57
Jensen Windsor (6) ... 58
Oliver James (6) ... 58
Taylor White (7) ... 59
Kyle Lowes (7) ... 59
Áine Lippolis (7) ... 60
Jack Watts (6) ... 60
Ethan Codd (7) ... 61
Jake Howarth (6) ... 61
Max Simpson (6) ... 62
Vincent McRae (6) ... 62

Danika Marks (6) ... 63
Tianna Coy (5) ... 63
Archie Murray (6) ... 64
Ben Ailsby (5) ... 64
Jacob Brown (5) ... 65
Nicole Meik (6) ... 65
Elise Guthrie (6) ... 66
Elise Roper (6) ... 66
Alice Pridgeon (6) ... 67
Archie Pridgeon (6) ... 67
Layton White (6) ... 68
Oliver Arnold (6) ... 68
Ellie Chambers (5) ... 69

Keelby Primary School, Keelby
Oliver Hill (6) ... 69
Laura Thomas (7) ... 70
Macey Sixsmith (7) ... 70
Rohanna Ede (7) ... 71
Lauren Jackson (7) ... 71
Megan Elliott (7) ... 72
Ebony Moffat (6) ... 72
Charlotte Bacon (7) ... 73

Maesbury Primary School, Oswestry
Charlie Fletcher (6) ... 73
Rebecca Owen (7) ... 74
Rhys Thomas (6) ... 74
Grace Perry (6) ... 75
Lucy Arrowsmith (7) ... 75

St Chad's Catholic Primary School, Sedgley
Benjamin Di Terlizzi (5) ... 76
Allicia Argueta (5) ... 76
Luca Mario (6) ... 77
Summer Louise Davies (5) ... 77
Dominic Simpson (5) ... 78
Rebecca Edwards (6) ... 78
Isabella Everall (5) ... 79
Noah Hagans (6) ... 79
Liberty (5) ... 80
Siobhan McSweeney (6) ... 80
Danny Joseph John (5) ... 81
Stanley Stokes (6) ... 81
Aoife Kent-Smith (5) ... 82

St George's CE Primary School, Swadlincote
Georgia Beattie (5) 82
Amelia Taylor (5) 83
Ella Dingley (6) 83
Aaliyah Wall (6) 84
Joshua Fisher (6) 84
Harvey Warren (6) 85
Jessica Gough (6) 85
Kiera Wheatcroft (6) 86
Hannah Greenwood (5) 86
Jai Evans (6) 87
Kallum Avery-Smith (6) 87
Aimee Decamps (6) 88
Emily Matkin (6) 88
Joshua Ogden (6) 89
Keegan Mulholland (5) 89
Amelie Fugiel Morris (6) 90
Natasha McInerney (6) 90
Fenton Wray (6) 91
Maisie Simpson (6) 91

St James' Preparatory School, Grimsby
Sofia Chacón-Tuke (7) 92
Teddy Woodhouse (7) 92
Harrison Gillett (7) 93
Amélia Lambert (7) 93
Sadhbh O'Sullivan (5) 94
Savannah Bradley (6) 94

St Lawrence CE (VA) Primary School, Napton
Matthew Darville (6) 95
Charlie Parsons (6) 95
Sinead Gillick (6) 96
Chanel Oliver (5) 96
Amelia Line (5) 97
Jay Hilton (6) 97
Harry Orton (6) 98
John Sharlot (7) 98
Jack Field (6) 99
Catherine Bouverie-Brine (6) 99
Jay Ramsay (6) 100

Springfield House Special School, Solihull
Jack Travis (6) 100
Leighton Oseman (5) 101
Beren Alesbrook-Wain (6) 101
Kieran Doyle (7) 102

Tibberton First School, Droitwich
Mia Bowen (6) 102
Torr Strange (6) 103
Blythe Kirkpatrick (7) 103
Ross Clews (6) 104
Jake Clews (5) 104
Charlie Hemming (6) 105
Reuben Hey (6) 105
Georgie Lewis (6) 106
Ben Darby (7) 106
Harvey Newman (6) 107
Katie Vertigen (6) 107

Whitwell Primary School, Whitwell
Maddison Johnson (6) 108
Nathan Skinner (7) 109
Lewis Longden (7) 110
Joel Whittaker Naylor (6) 111
Cain Womble (6) 112
Louise Machin (7) 113
Lucy Forrest (7) 114
Abbie Shiwell (7) 115
Dylan Ryles 116
Jaydan Plummer (6) 117
Harvey Baker (6) 118
Harvey Spencer (6) 119
Taylor Atkinson (7) 120
Harvey Smith (6) 121
Mollie Godley (6) 122
Lydia Allen (7) 123
Lucy McKnight (7) 124
Caitlin Mather (7) 125

Wistanstow CE Primary School, Craven Arms
Lucy Orme (5) 126
Yousef Aokal (6) 126
Aaron Northwood (5) 127

Daniel Liebrecht (6) 127
Kaitlyn Orme (6) 128
Lewis Key (5) 128
Isobel Hatton (5) 129
Joanna Selley (7) 129
Tilly Pinches (6) 130
Tegan Pinches (7) 130

Wyberton Primary School, Boston

Andrew Smith (6) 131
Joel Wilson (7) 131
James Dawson (7) 132
Chloe Paddison (7) 132
Bethany Bradley (6) 133
Caitlin Charlesworth (7) 133
Harry Newell (7) 134
Aaron Kirkham (7) 134
Molly Andrew (7) 135
Henry Ellis (7) 135
Zac Baldry (6) 136
Joshua Comrie (6) 136
Charlie Summerland (6) 137
Nayana Gash (7) 137
Elliot Wilson (6) 138
Thomas Noone (7) 138
Lianne Wilkinson (6) 139
Max Doherty (6) 139
Jake Smith (6) 140
Tyler Robinson (5) 140
Madaline Pearson (5) 141
Abigail Winrow (6) 141
Summer Houlden-Steers (5) 142
Jamie Lawrence (6) 142
Osian Joyce (6) 143
Cheila Vidrago 143
Ashley Strickland (6) 144

The Poems

My First Acrostic - The East & West Midlands

Robin

R obins are red and brown
O range beaks
B usy pecking
I n spring they have baby robins
N esting in the garden.

Sophia Field (7)

Seasons

S pring has got flowers
E veryone knows that
A ball of white thing is snow
S ummer is hot
O ctober is autumn
N ever play in the summer too much
S now is very cold.

Denisa Krasniqi (7)
Alvaston Junior Community School, Derby

Bethany

B eautiful
E asy to get along with
T otally cute
H appy as can be
A ccidents all the time!
N utty
Y oung

A cting all the time
N aughty (sometimes)
N ice to Mummy
E xcitable

H opelessly in love with cats
A nd charming
Y elling all the time
W illing to help
A ngry sometimes
R eally likes riding bikes
D oes like animals.

Bethany Hayward (6)
Bishopton Primary School, Stratford Upon Avon

My First Acrostic - The East & West Midlands

Frankie Dettori

F ine jockey
R ides horses
A lways tries his best
N ever gives up
K eeps on wining races
I deal rider
E njoys Arsenal football team

D oes not like small aeroplanes
E ats fruit for his breakfast
T alks to the horses
T hinks Ascot is the best racecourse
O nly jumps off a horse if he wins
R ode some donkeys in his past
I s always smiling.

Reece Stanley (7)
Bishopton Primary School, Stratford Upon Avon

My Dad

D oes work
A t home he plays
D oes jobs.

Jamie Storey (6)
Bishopton Primary School, Stratford Upon Avon

Maddy

M addy and Amy
A nd Bonnie
D oing painting
D oing colouring
Y et when we grow up, we'll still be friends.

Madeline Macleod (7)
Bishopton Primary School, Stratford Upon Avon

Train

T rain-tastic
R iding the rails
A lways puffing
I n and out of the station
N early always on time.

Jack Smith (6)
Bishopton Primary School, Stratford Upon Avon

My First Acrostic - The East & West Midlands

Joshua

J umps
O ff the cliffs
S leeps all the night
H as a friend
U p and over the mountain
A lways helps

W alks the dog
A lways needs help
S ays no
L ikes ice cream
E njoys football
Y ells loudly!

Joshua Wasley (6)
Bishopton Primary School, Stratford Upon Avon

Amy Harris

A lways playing
M y best friend is Maddy
Y ummy strawberries are the best fruit

H SM2 is my favourite film
A urora is my favourite princess
R eady to learn
R emember to do my homework
I love my family
S kipping is what I like to do.

Amy Harris (7)
Bishopton Primary School, Stratford Upon Avon

Tiger

T ough and strong
I rresponsible because it eats meat
G rowls like a lion
E ats antelope
R uns very fast.

Emma Dyke (7)
Bishopton Primary School, Stratford Upon Avon

My First Acrostic - The East & West Midlands

Spring

S unny days
P retty flowers
R oses swaying
I love spring
N ewborn babies
G ranting wishes.

Jaaouine Imane (7)
Bishopton Primary School, Stratford Upon Avon

Doctor Who

D aleks are very bad
R ose was a good companion
W ho travelled with the Doctor
H e lives in a TARDIS
O od are very good.

Jake Hartnett (7)
Bishopton Primary School, Stratford Upon Avon

Alyssa

A lyssa is kind and brings a smile to the day.
L istening carefully to what her friends say.
Y ou would like to be me.
S inging and laughing all day long.
S howing everyone what dance I can do.
A lways learning something new.

Alyssa Jardim (6)
Bournebrook CE Primary School, Fillongley

Snakey Seth

S nakey Seth slithers around
E very day he turns round
T o see his prey
H e always gets his tasty meal.

Seth Nesbitt (6)
Bournebrook CE Primary School, Fillongley

My First Acrostic - The East & West Midlands

Jumping Jake

J umping Jake is always very bouncy
A nd very noisy when he is bouncing like a
K angaroo. He is always
E ager in all that we do.

Jake James-Preece (7)
Bournebrook CE Primary School, Fillongley

Dangerous Daniel

D angerous Daniel is so strong. I can pull
A train that is so long
N one of my friends can believe it
I can't even believe it myself
E veryone is amazed with me
L ife is like a dream to me.

Daniel Sutton (7)
Bournebrook CE Primary School, Fillongley

Emma

E mma eats lots of treats, she
M unches and crunches at the boiled sweets
M aybe one day her teeth with fall out
A nd she will be sad and very mad.

Emma Newcombe (6)
Bournebrook CE Primary School, Fillongley

Horsey Haidee

H orsey Haidee loves horses
A nd ponies
I love all animals too.
D angerous animals I don't like. I am
E xcellent at riding horses and get
E xcited when I do jumping.

Haidee Davies (7)
Bournebrook CE Primary School, Fillongley

My First Acrostic - The East & West Midlands

Holly

H aving a dog is special to me, we
O ften take long walks together and look at the
L ovely scenery. Every day I
L ove her more and more.
Y ou would love to meet Sophie and she would give her paw.

Holly Guise (7)
Bournebrook CE Primary School, Fillongley

Strong Sam

S trong Sam
A nd angry Sam
M ischief Sam
U seful Sam
E erie Sam and
L ovely Sam.

Samuel Billington (6)
Bournebrook CE Primary School, Fillongley

Rebecca

R ebecca is beautiful and very, very kind.
E very day in class she uses her mind. Her nickname is
B ecky, all her friends call her that.
E veryone likes her because she laughs and plays
C hatting her friends and smiling always
C atching and shouting whilst having lots of fun
A nd jumping and skipping in the sun.

Rebecca Smith (6)
Bournebrook CE Primary School, Fillongley

Kind Katelyn

K ind Katelyn is very clever, I am
A lways so patient and so witty. I am
T alented at horse riding
E specially at trotting around the field
L ong days I spend riding
Y ou would love to join me
N ever fear, clever Katelyn is here.

Katelyn Acton (7)
Bournebrook CE Primary School, Fillongley

My First Acrostic - **The East & West Midlands**

Marshmallow Michael

M arshmallow Michael all squidgy and squashy
I know I am in danger of being eaten
C an you see me hiding in the bottom of the packet?
H ungry people with big glary eyes
A nd a big watery mouth and a big rumbly belly
E verybody wants a marshmallow just like me
L ovely and tasty just like me. I jumped out of
the packet and said, 'Don't eat me!'

Michael Whitehouse (6)
Bournebrook CE Primary School, Fillongley

Reefy Roger

R eefy Roger likes bouncing and jumping about
E very day is the same, spinning around and around
E verybody likes me, I have lots of fun with friends
F unny me, I always giggle with glee.

Reef Billingham (6)
Bournebrook CE Primary School, Fillongley

Elephant Ella

E lephant Ella likes playing with water. I
L ike to spray everyone and giggle with glee
L aughing and joking all day long
A lways singing a joyful song.

Ella Lawrence (7)
Bournebrook CE Primary School, Fillongley

Transport

T rains chugging on the tracks
R acing
A bout
N oisy and
S melly
P lanes flying
O ver clouds
R ockets zoom
T ransport.

Owen Keelan (6)
Church Vale Primary School, Warsop

My First Acrostic – The East & West Midlands

Transport

T rains going past
R acing along the road
A eroplanes flying people to
N ew lands
S hips sailing on the seas
P olice cars
O vertaking
R ushing
T o arrest.

Keaton Ellis (7)
Church Vale Primary School, Warsop

Transport

T ractors on the
R oad
A nd
N ow in the fields.
S hips in the
P ort sailing
O ver sea.
R ocks zooming
T o space.

Caitlin Payne (7)
Church Vale Primary School, Warsop

Transport

T rain
R ushing
A long the track
N oisy car riding along the road
S hips going into the sea
P eople crossing
O ver the
R oad
T ransport.

Tate O'Neill (7)
Church Vale Primary School, Warsop

Transport

T ruck and lorry
R ide on the road.
A ir balloon.
N o noise.
S ilent
P ackages in vans all
O ver the world.
R ocket.
T ransport.

Mazie Piontek (6)
Church Vale Primary School, Warsop

My First Acrostic - The East & West Midlands

Transport

T ractors chugging in the fields
R ipping soil.
A nimals run.
N oisy planes fly high above.
S peedboats racing.
P eople rushing
O ver the bridges
R oller coaster, aeroplanes, air balloon and cars.
T ransport.

Leyah Swinn (7)
Church Vale Primary School, Warsop

Transport

T rucks
R ushing past.
A nimals creeping in the long grass.
N ot a
S ound in the night.
P eople running along the path.
O ver the bridge comes a car
R ushing to get home quick.
T hese are all types of transport!

Eloise O'Donnell (6)
Church Vale Primary School, Warsop

Transport

T rucks and lorries
R acing and rushing
A ir balloon floats across the sky
N orth to
S outh
P ackages and parcels in vans all
O ver the world.
R ocket truck
T ransport.

Katie Warren (6)
Church Vale Primary School, Warsop

Transport

T ransport
R oads are busy, busy
A lot of post on a truck
N avy
S hip
P uffing and chugging
O ver the sea
R ushing
T raffic.

Katie Morris (6)
Church Vale Primary School, Warsop

My First Acrostic – The East & West Midlands

Transport

T ractors running on the mud.
R ushing
A round.
N oisy and smelly.
S hips sailing
P ort to port.
O pen
R oads.
T ransport.

Annice Murphy (6)
Church Vale Primary School, Warsop

Transport

T ractor running on the mud
R ockets zooming into space
A racing car speeding
N oisy and loud
S hips sailing
P lanes flying
O ver the cars
R ushing around
T raffic.

Joey Root (6)
Church Vale Primary School, Warsop

Transport

T ransport
R ocket zooming
A ir balloon floating
N o noise
S hips on the sea
P lanes flying
O ver
R ushing
T raffic.

Joseph Bramley Bird (6)
Church Vale Primary School, Warsop

Terrific Tilly

T errific Tilly
I nteresting Tilly
L ovely Tilly
L ucky Tilly
Y es Tilly is my friend.

Mia Montgomery (7)
Coomb Briggs Primary School, Immingham

My First Acrostic – The East & West Midlands

Abbie

A bbie is interesting.
B eautiful Abbie is beautiful.
B egging Abbie.
I nggram is Abbie's favourite name.
E njoyable Abbie.

Abbie is my friend.

Rhiannon Graves (7)
Coomb Briggs Primary School, Immingham

Lovely Olivia

O nly Olivia
L ovely Olivia
I nteresting Olivia
V iolet is my nearest favourite colour
I ncredible
A mazing Olivia.

Olivia Black (7)
Coomb Briggs Primary School, Immingham

Chirpy Charlie

C harlie is fast like a train
H elpful
A ngry
R ed is his favourite colour
L ovely Charlie
I ncredible
E xcellent Charlie.

Charlie Bates (6) & Lewis Knox
Coomb Briggs Primary School, Immingham

Excellent Eloise

E njoy
L ovely
O wls are my favourite animal
I nteresting
S is the 5th letter in my name
E xcellent.

Eloise Owens (7)
Coomb Briggs Primary School, Immingham

My First Acrostic - The East & West Midlands

Rainforest

R eally hot place.
A nimals are losing their homes.
I n danger of people.
N ice place to be.
F or people to enjoy.
O ther people destroy it.
R ubbish is getting thrown in.
E veryone loves it.
S ave the animals.
T he people are hurting the animals.

Ashleigh Barley (7)
Frodingham Infant School, Scunthorpe

Arctic

A lways a cold place to be.
R eally take care of the animals.
C an you help?
T he polar bears are dying.
I f you can help do it please.
C an you help the polar bears please?

Teri Pell (6)
Frodingham Infant School, Scunthorpe

Rainforest

R eally wet.
A nimals' homes are getting destroyed.
I nteresting animals are getting hurt.
N ot helping the environment.
F orest getting burnt down.
O ffer please.
R emoving the trees.
E nvironment getting worse.
S o many people are letting them die.
T he people are heating the world for them.

Reece Fullerton (7)
Frodingham Infant School, Scunthorpe

Arctic

A really cold place
R eally small icebergs because of the pollution
C ities are causing the pollution
T he polar bears are dying every day, every night
I think we can do better
C aring for our planet is everyone's job.

Joshua Brader (7)
Frodingham Infant School, Scunthorpe

My First Acrostic - **The East & West Midlands**

Rainforest

R emoving our trees
A nimals are dying, please help us
I nteresting animals are getting hurt
N ot helping the environment
F orests are being burnt down and causing fires
O ffer to help please
R eally upsetting for us and animals
E nvironment is getting destroyed
S o many people are letting the animals down
T he people are heating the world.

Tyler Marshall (7)
Frodingham Infant School, Scunthorpe

Arctic

A lways a cold place to be
R eally need to help the animals
C ome and take care of the Arctic
T ry to stop pollution
I ce is melting away
C an you stop damaging the Arctic?

Hannah Jordan (7)
Frodingham Infant School, Scunthorpe

Arctic

A nimals are dying, please help us.
R eally wet and cold place to be.
C ome and help us save animals.
T iny babies don't want to die.
I f you can adopt a polar bear you're welcome.
C ome and help animals. Thank you.

George McLean (7)
Frodingham Infant School, Scunthorpe

Arctic

A nimals like polar bears have no home.
R eally cold place to be.
C ome and help the polar bears.
T he people are heating the world.
I n danger of animals dying.
C ome and help the world.

Ellie Mae Holmes (6)
Frodingham Infant School, Scunthorpe

My First Acrostic - The East & West Midlands

Arctic

A nimals live on ice
R eally polar bears will soon die
C old place to be
T he ice is melting
I ce is melting, where are the homes?
C ome and help!

Brandon Poole (7)
Frodingham Infant School, Scunthorpe

Arctic

A very cold place.
R eally white everywhere.
C ome save the polar bears.
T oo hot for the polar bears.
I want to help them.
C ome on help the animals.

Bethany Patrick (7)
Frodingham Infant School, Scunthorpe

Rainforest

R euse paper, tins and plastic.
A nimals are becoming extinct.
I will help them, will you?
N eed your help at once.
F urry creatures enjoy the trees.
O thers will help, please can you?
R eally important.
E ven babies die.
S ave the forest and animals!
T hey might go before you help.

Holly Jacklin (7)
Frodingham Infant School, Scunthorpe

Arctic

A ll the ice is melting.
R eally, really cold.
C ome and save the polar bear.
T ake care of the polar bear.
I ce is turning into water.
C ome and save our world today.

Jack Parratt Guntrip (6)
Frodingham Infant School, Scunthorpe

My First Acrostic - The East & West Midlands

Coral Reef

C an you stop breaking the coral?
O ctopuses are scared.
R ainbow fish are dying.
A ll the fish are dying.
L ots of crabs.

R eally dirty water.
E veryone stop breaking coral.
E very creature in the ocean is special.
F ind a way to save them.

Ciaran Sykes (7)
Frodingham Infant School, Scunthorpe

Arctic

A frozen land.
R eally sad if it disappears.
C ruel people destroying the Earth.
T urn off your power.
I f you don't it will be too late.
C are.

Kieran Busby (6)
Frodingham Infant School, Scunthorpe

Climate Change

C are for our world
L ook after it
I ce is melted by the sun
M any animals' habitats are destroyed
A nimals are endangered
T rees are being chopped down
E veryone should find out more

C hange the world
H elp the animals
A lways recycle
N ever put rubbish in the sea
G row new trees
E verybody should walk or ride bikes.

Jasmine Calder (6)
Frodingham Infant School, Scunthorpe

My First Acrostic - **The East & West Midlands**

Global Warming

G et help to recycle
L itter must go in the bin.
O ur world needs caring for.
B e kind and rescue the animals.
A nimals need their habitat to survive.
L ots of animals are becoming endangered.

W e can help by going on a bus or a train.
A nimals are becoming extinct.
R ainforest habitats are getting destroyed.
M aking too much smoke.
I t can make water disappear.
N ot a nice place.
G et out of your chair and help!

Wesley Jay Pearce (7)
Frodingham Infant School, Scunthorpe

The Earth

T reat the world carefully!
H abitats are disappearing
E verywhere.

E arth is suffocating extremely slowly.
A nimals are in forests so stop chopping forests down.
R eusing things will help animals.
T ake rubbish to the dump because recycling helps.
H elp keep the world a nice place to be.

Hannah Whittaker (6)
Frodingham Infant School, Scunthorpe

Rainforest

R eally fast animals
A ll the trees are important
I nteresting creatures
N ever ruin our world
F amilies of monkeys
O rang-utans!
R ed parrot
E xtra special
S piders
T igers.

Reece Moir (6)
Frodingham Infant School, Scunthorpe

My First Acrostic - The East & West Midlands

Pollution

P erhaps we could stop throwing rubbish into the sea.
O ur habitats are being destroyed.
L ove and care for our Earth.
L ots of smoke coming out of cars!
U nfortunately people are destroying the Earth.
T ime to clean up the rubbish.
I will do it, will you?
O ur habitats are being destroyed by people.
N obody should damage the Earth.

Nathan Ferguson (7)
Frodingham Infant School, Scunthorpe

Pollution

P lease help us
O ut!
L ove plants
L ots of animals are endangered
U nfortunately people pour pollution into the sea!
T reat the world better.
I think we should make a change.
O ur factories are making carbon dioxide.
N ever litter.

Katie Craven (7)
Frodingham Infant School, Scunthorpe

Rainforest

R aindrops pitter-pattering.
A nimals like to live here.
I love animals.
N ever hurt animals.
F rogs, birds and monkeys live in the trees.
O ur animals are dying in the rainforest.
R ainforests are dangerous and scary because there are gorillas.
E xcellent animals.
S ave the rainforests.
T hey are special.

Leah Sweeting (7)
Frodingham Infant School, Scunthorpe

My First Acrostic - The East & West Midlands

Coral Reef

C urly and wiggly, a wonderful habitat for the fish.
O ur world is suffering because coral reefs are getting destroyed.
R ubbish is thrown in it and it's killing the animals.
A lovely strange environment.
L ike seaweed.

R emember not to spoil this wonderful place.
E xtremely nice to the starfish.
E legantly swishes from side to side.
F ish swim everywhere, please save them.
S ick animals are dying because we are throwing rubbish in the coral reefs.

Aberam Prathaban (6)
Frodingham Infant School, Scunthorpe

The Arctic

T he ice is melting, the penguins are disappearing.

H elp

E ndangered animals.

A nimals are in danger.

R escue them.

C ities are full of factories

T ake care of them polluting the world.

L ove the animals.

C are for the Arctic.

Corey Lewis (7)
Frodingham Infant School, Scunthorpe

Recycle

R ubbish is being thrown on the seashore.

E veryone can help.

C an you put it in the bin?

Y ou can recycle things.

C are for the Earth.

L ove the animals.

E veryone needs to pick this rubbish up.

Chloe Grierson (7)
Frodingham Infant School, Scunthorpe

My First Acrostic - The East & West Midlands

Rubbish

R ecycling is fantastic.
U nfortunately people throw rubbish in the sea.
B oxes are made out of cardboard, put it in the recycling bin.
B ottles go in the recycling bin.
I t's really, really great.
S ave our planet.
H undreds of animals have nowhere to live.

Fayaz Badruddoza (6)
Frodingham Infant School, Scunthorpe

The Arctic

T he ice is melting.
H elp animals.
E verybody must listen.

A polar bear lives here.
R eally beautiful penguins live here with their
C hicks.
T ry to not pollute.
I don't want them to disappear.
C hange!

Kacper Jakimowski (7)
Frodingham Infant School, Scunthorpe

The Arctic

The Arctic is getting destroyed.
Here in the Arctic polar bears and penguins live.
Everyone help us please, because the Arctic is melting.

Are you going to help us in the Arctic?
Rubbish is making the world horrible.
Can you help us please, please?
The Arctic is getting worse so help us.
I want to help them, do you?
Can we help them?

Ellie-Mae Jackson (6)
Frodingham Infant School, Scunthorpe

Rubbish

Rubbish everywhere.
Untidy world.
Bottles in the sea.
Birds are getting killed.
Ice is melting.
Save our planet.
How can we help?

Dylan Lovell (7)
Frodingham Infant School, Scunthorpe

My First Acrostic - The East & West Midlands

Sam

S am likes Lego
A nd Joe is my best friend.
M y favourite colour is red.

J elly is mad.
A nimals are nice.
C at is good.
K ings are silly.
S am likes crisps.
O ranges are yummy.
N athan is my brother.

Samuel Jackson (6)
Gosberton Community Primary School, Gosberton

Joseph

J elly likes jumping.
O ranges are horrible.
S ensible.
E lephants are big.
P uffins are perfect.
H amsters are hungry.

Joseph Cowling (5)
Gosberton Community Primary School, Gosberton

Maria

M aria likes making cakes
A sk questions
R abbits are nice
I like making chocolate
A lways keep the golden rules.

W orking
O range is my favourite colour.
O ranges are my favourite food.
D reaming is my favourite thing when I'm sleeping.
S tories are fun.

Maria Woods (6)
Gosberton Community Primary School, Gosberton

Levi

L evi is my name.
E aster eggs are
V ery yummy
I n my tummy.

Levi Tolson (6)
Gosberton Community Primary School, Gosberton

My First Acrostic - The East & West Midlands

Mellyssa

M akes mustard
E lephants stomp slowly
L ikes lollies
L ove you Mummy
Y oyo is my favourite toy
S lugs make me scream
S nakes are slimy
A nts tickle.

Mellyssa Doades (6)
Gosberton Community Primary School, Gosberton

Tia

T ia likes a rabbit
I t licks my hand
A ll the time.

Tia Leoni Shirley (5)
Gosberton Community Primary School, Gosberton

Joe

J oe likes jelly
O ctopus eats oats
E is my favourite letter

M akes cakes
A nts are my favourite animal
L ove beavers
T is for table
B is for bee
Y is for yoyo.

Joe Maltby (5)
Gosberton Community Primary School, Gosberton

Alex

A shark is in his bedroom
L auren went to the shops
E lla went to the park
eX tra kind to himself.

Alexander Stacey (6)
Gosberton Community Primary School, Gosberton

My First Acrostic - The East & West Midlands

Ella

E lephants are my favourite animals.
L ike making cakes.
L ions are frightening.
A nimals are different kinds I know.

E lle is my favourite friend.
V ans are slow.
E lla eats chocolate cake.
R abbits jump around.
E lephants are huge.
S am is so silly.
T ia is nice.

Ella Everest (6)
Gosberton Community Primary School, Gosberton

Cormac's Life

C ormac is my name and I like to write
O range is my favourite colour because it is bright
R unning stitch is my favourite because I am good
M aths is my favourite subject, I am a fan
A lways try to be helpful when I can
C olourful stuff makes me happy and jolly.

Cormac Wolstenholme (6)
Heathfield School, Kidderminster

My World

H annah is my name
A nd I love my two best friends
N uts is my teddy Hazel, she is a teddy squirrel
N ew girl is coming next week
A lice tries to be good
H aving presents on Christmas Day

B en is a good friend to have
A nd he comes and plays when he's got nothing to do
K issing my mummy and daddy
E very night before I go to bed
R abbits are my favourite pets, so are dogs.

Hannah Baker (6)
Heathfield School, Kidderminster

My First Acrostic - The East & West Midlands

Jack Wharton

J ack Wharton is nice
A nd is really
C ool. He is
K een to

W alk across the world.
H e could go through the
A ctive wood.
R iding on his bike, or he could
T ry to go
O n a skidoo to the
N orth Pole.

Jack Wharton (6)
Heathfield School, Kidderminster

What I Like

D J3K is my favourite computer game
A rmour is my favourite thing to see, it is shiny and protects you from pain.
R oald Dahl books are my favourite stories, they are interesting.
C orn is my favourite food because it is sweet.
Y aks are my favourite animals because they have horns and hard feet.

Darcy Scott Worrall (7)
Heathfield School, Kidderminster

Sebastian

S ebastian likes to
E at. He is a
B oy
A nd he is
S ix years old. He likes
T o play on the computer.
I n the night he steals
A pples.
N ow he plays on the little computer.

Sebastian Mitchell (6)
Heathfield School, Kidderminster

My First Acrostic – **The East & West Midlands**

Joseph's Poem

J oseph Hallowell has
O nly one sister. He is
S ix years old. He likes to
E at chips. He has a
P et cat who sleeps in a
H uge

H at
A nd he likes to tell jokes because he
L ikes
L aughing
O ut loud. He
W ants
E veryone to
L augh out
L oud too.

Joseph Hallowell (6)
Heathfield School, Kidderminster

Leah Is Helpful

L eah Tidmarsh
E ats a lot of food. She is
A lways kind and
H elpful to people. She loves all her friends

T oo.
I love my
D ad and
M um
A nd they love me
R eally they do.
S o Leah Tidmarsh is always a
H appy, friendly girl.

Leah Tidmarsh (6)
Heathfield School, Kidderminster

My First Acrostic - The East & West Midlands

All About Me

O liver Bailey
L ikes to play
I nside his house, he is
V ery
E nergetic and is
R eally good on his box. He has

B lue eyes and he is always
A ctive in the day, but
I n bed he is always
L azy and likes to
E at mash because it is
Y ummy.

Oliver Bailey (6)
Heathfield School, Kidderminster

Lucy's Cat

L ucy Newton wears her
U niform. She has three
C ats, one is bright
Y ellow and does

N ot like to
E at the
W rong food. The two other cats
T ry to give him the right name
O ne day I got my cats and
N ow they are so *big!*

Lucy Newton (6)
Heathfield School, Kidderminster

My First Acrostic - **The East & West Midlands**

All About Me

E vie Tonks is a
V ery good girl. She
I s very
E nergetic. She is never in

T rouble. She loves
O ranges. She has a cute
N ose. She has
K nobbly knees and a great big
S mile.

Evie Tonks (6)
Heathfield School, Kidderminster

Molly Loves Lollipops

M olly Mae Hall
O ne day
L aughed out loud. She
L oves anything
Y ellow.

M olly Mae Hall
A nd
E vie Tonks

H ad
A great big
L ollipop in
L ondon.

Molly Mae Hall (5)
Heathfield School, Kidderminster

My First Acrostic – The East & West Midlands

Eve Sinclair-Hall

E ve Sinclair-Hall is
V ery nice.
E very day

S he
I s
N ice and
C lever, but sometimes
L azy and
A lways plays
I nside
R eading, and is
-
H appy all the time
A nd loves
L azing about in the
L ovely long grass.

Eve Sinclair-Hall (5)
Heathfield School, Kidderminster

The Zoo

E mily Diaz's
M um and dad are
I nside and are
L aughing at Dad's jokes. I like
Y ellow.

D ad helps me with my work
I n the garden
A nd me and my sister go to see
Z ebras in the zoo.

Emily Diaz (5)
Heathfield School, Kidderminster

Football

R obbie Cox ran
O nto the pitch.
B irmingham City.
B en loves Manchester United and
I love Manchester United too.
E lephants spray water.

C himpanzees swing
O n trees. I love
X Factor.

Robert Cox (5)
Heathfield School, Kidderminster

My First Acrostic - The East & West Midlands

The Naughty Boy

B rooklyn Taylor and
R obbie Cox and
O liver Bailey said
O K to the
K ing. They all
L oved playing with a
Y oyo. A
N aughty boy said, 'Go away.'

Brooklyn Taylor (6)
Heathfield School, Kidderminster

Seasons - Spring

S ee the baby animals.
P rimroses growing.
R obins singing.
I n the swimming pool.
N ice sunny days.
G rass is growing.

Iona Jones (6)
Huttoft Primary School, Alford

Seasons – Spring

S pring is here now.
P urple flowers are starting to bloom.
R ainy days sometimes.
I t is time for things to grow.
N ice flowers are growing.
G et up and go outside and play.

Zoe Burton (6)
Huttoft Primary School, Alford

Seasons – Spring

S pring is fun
P retty flowers grow
R ain on plants
I t is green
N ow new baby animals are born
G et to see bunnies.

Emily Barker (6)
Huttoft Primary School, Alford

My First Acrostic - **The East & West Midlands**

Seasons – Spring

S un is hot.
P otatoes are growing.
R ainy days.
I am running outside.
N ow the sun is out.
G rass is growing longer.

Jacob Skinner (7)
Huttoft Primary School, Alford

Spring

S ee the lambs and chicks in springtime.
P retty flowers are growing.
R abbits are running.
I ce cream is wanted by lots of kids.
N ests are up in the trees.
G ates are opening at hotels.

Michelle Virgo (7)
Huttoft Primary School, Alford

Seasons - Spring

S pring is sunny.
P rimroses growing.
R oses are growing in the playground.
I t's getting warmer today.
N ew leaves growing on the tree.
G rowing new flowers in the playground.

Jensen Windsor (6)
Huttoft Primary School, Alford

Seasons - Spring

S unny days.
P laying in the sandpit.
R abbits are jumping.
I t is getting warmer.
N ow we are on the trampoline.
G rowing lawn.

Oliver James (6)
Huttoft Primary School, Alford

My First Acrostic - The East & West Midlands

Spring

S unny days are coming
P laying in the garden is fun
R unning and jumping rabbits
I t is getting warmer
N ew flowers are growing
G rowing leaves on the tree.

Taylor White (7)
Huttoft Primary School, Alford

Seasons - Summer

S ummer is the time when the sun is out.
U p, up in the clear blue sky.
M ost trees are getting leaves.
M ake the paddling pool.
E very day I go to the beach.
R est in the garden.

Kyle Lowes (7)
Huttoft Primary School, Alford

Winter

Winter is cold.
In winter there's no leaves on the trees.
Not all leaves are off the trees, holly leaves aren't.
There's no flowers in winter.
Even my sister, Siobhán, comes round for winter.
Right now it's time for sleep, did you know that in winter it's hot at night.

Áine Lippolis (7)
Huttoft Primary School, Alford

Hot

Here is the sun
Off comes my jumper
To the park I go.

Jack Watts (6)
Huttoft Primary School, Alford

My First Acrostic - The East & West Midlands

Summer

S ummer is a nice day
U p in the sky is a shiny sun
M ore flowers are getting ready to grow
M any flowers are opening up
E very day is getting hotter
R ed apples are growing on the trees.

Ethan Codd (7)
Huttoft Primary School, Alford

Autumn

A way the leaves fall
U p in the trees the leaves are falling
T rees have leaves
U nder the leaves are bugs
M any leaves are here
N ot just leaves!

Jake Howarth (6)
Huttoft Primary School, Alford

Weather - Sunny

- **S** ee the sun
- **U** p in the sky
- **N** ot on the ground
- **N** ow the sun is shining
- **Y** ou can play.

Max Simpson (6)
Huttoft Primary School, Alford

Weather - Sun

- **S** un so bright
- **U** p so high
- **N** ice day to play.

Vincent McRae (6)
Huttoft Primary School, Alford

My First Acrostic - The East & West Midlands

Weather - Wind

W ind is cold
I t blows
N ow there are leaves
D ropping from the trees.

Danika Marks (6)
Huttoft Primary School, Alford

Weather - Sun

S un so bright
U p in the sky
N ow put your sunglasses on.

Tianna Coy (5)
Huttoft Primary School, Alford

Sun

S un is really hot
U mbrella is needed
N ice to play with my dog.

Archie Murray (6)
Huttoft Primary School, Alford

Weather - Wind

W indy weather
I n my big garden
N ow I put my coat on
D ig a hole for a plant.

Ben Ailsby (5)
Huttoft Primary School, Alford

My First Acrostic - The East & West Midlands

Weather - Hail

H ard hail
A ll in my face
I n my eyes
L oud in the sky.

Jacob Brown (5)
Huttoft Primary School, Alford

Weather - Sun

S un in the sky
U nder the sun
N ice weather.

Nicole Meik (6)
Huttoft Primary School, Alford

Weather - Sunny

S it in the sun
U nder the sea
N ice to swim
N ow I go on holiday
Y ou are a nice sun.

Elise Guthrie (6)
Huttoft Primary School, Alford

Weather - Sun

S unny day
U p in the sky
N ice day to play.

Elise Roper (6)
Huttoft Primary School, Alford

My First Acrostic - The East & West Midlands

Weather - Snow

S now is fun
N ot when it is cold
O ut in the garden
W e will play.

Alice Pridgeon (6)
Huttoft Primary School, Alford

Weather - Sun

S un is bright
U p in the sky
N ice to have an ice cream.

Archie Pridgeon (6)
Huttoft Primary School, Alford

Weather – Snow

S it in the snow
N ow I am wet
O ut in the garden
W e make a snowman.

Layton White (6)
Huttoft Primary School, Alford

Weather – Sun

S un is really hot
U nder the ground it is cold
N o it's not going to rain.

Oliver Arnold (6)
Huttoft Primary School, Alford

My First Acrostic - The East & West Midlands

Weather - Sun

S un is very, very hot
U se a sun hat to keep you cool
N ice to get my water slide out.

Ellie Chambers (5)
Huttoft Primary School, Alford

Recycling

R ecycle tins for the recycling people to collect.
E verything goes to a dump.
C ollect different things to recycle.
Y ou can recycle lots of different things.
C ollect lots of different things for the environment.
L ife would be different without recycling.
E veryone, everyone, please recycle to save our planet!

Oliver Hill (6)
Keelby Primary School, Keelby

Recycling

R ecycle bottles, cans and glass.
E verything cannot be recycled because if you draw a picture and give it to someone it can still be recycled.
C ollect things that go in the recycling bin.
Y ou have to recycle things because if you don't you will have a pile of rubbish.
C ans can be recycled because if you don't you will have a pile of rubbish.
L eaving things that need to be recycled is very naughty.
E very piece of paper can be recycled.

Laura Thomas (7)
Keelby Primary School, Keelby

Recycling

R ecycle bottles, glass, tins, but not everything can be recycled.
E verything cannot be recycled because they might not be the right things.
C hildren can recycle some of their pictures too.
Y ou can recycle bottles as well.
C an recycle these things to help save our planet.
L etters can go in the recycle bin.
E verything cannot be recycled because they are not the right things.

Macey Sixsmith (7)
Keelby Primary School, Keelby

My First Acrostic - The East & West Midlands

Recycling

R ecycling is important
E verything cannot be recycled
C ollect everything that should go in the recycling bin
Y ou should recycle so that there are not humungous heaps of rubbish
C ollect everything that should go in like bottles and cans.
L ots of things should go in the recycling bin.
E verything that is recyclable goes in the recycling bin.
Help us now!

Rohanna Ede (7)
Keelby Primary School, Keelby

Recycling

R ecycle tin cans and other things like bottles, tubes and newspapers.
E veryone has to try to recycle every day.
C an you recycle your things? It helps the environment.
Y ou can do it every day, try it.
C an you help the environment?
L earn to recycle, it is good for the world, if you don't the world will be like a dump.
E veryone can help. *Now!*

Lauren Jackson (7)
Keelby Primary School, Keelby

Recycling

R ecycling is fun to do!
E very tin and bottle can be recycled.
C ollect all the cardboard boxes.
Y ou can recycle your dad's newspaper.
C an you recycle to save our planet?
L ife will get worse if you don't recycle because the world will be covered in junk!
E veryone has to recycle to save the world today!

Megan Elliott (7)
Keelby Primary School, Keelby

Recycling

R ubbish does not always go in the recycle bin.
E verything that is like when you got it can go in the recycle bin.
C lean your rubbish up like tins, newspapers, wood and toilet rolls.
Y ou do not recycle wool or plastic bags.
C lever bugs sometimes eat your recycled things.
L itter goes into big holes, if you do not recycle they will fill up too high.
E very bit of recycled material is made into different things over and over again.

Ebony Moffat (6)
Keelby Primary School, Keelby

My First Acrostic - The East & West Midlands

Recycling

R ecycling things can make things.
E ven bottles, tins, plastic and glass can go in the recycling bin.
C ollect lots of things that you can recycle.
Y oung children can recycle their old pictures.
C ollecting recycling things can help the environment because then we won't have lots of rubbish all over the country.
L ots of things can be recycled, but not all things.
E verything cannot be recycled, like old clocks and cars.

Please, please recycle things to help save our planet from rubbish.

Charlotte Bacon (7)
Keelby Primary School, Keelby

Charlie

C lever
H elps others
A nice person
R eally good boy
L ikes cucumber
I ncredible boy
E lephant liker.

Charlie Fletcher (6)
Maesbury Primary School, Oswestry

Rebecca

- **R** unning all day
- **E** ating five a day
- **B** ouncing balls
- **E** ating Easter eggs
- **C** uddling kittens
- **C** ycling about
- **A** cting at Stagecoach.

Rebecca Owen (7)
Maesbury Primary School, Oswestry

Rhys

- **R** ascal boy
- **H** as a messy room
- **Y** ellow lover
- **S** hell lover.

Rhys Thomas (6)
Maesbury Primary School, Oswestry

My First Acrostic - The East & West Midlands

Grace

G iddy half hour every day
R uns very fast
A funny friend
C url at the bottom of my hair
E ats a lot of food.

Grace Perry (6)
Maesbury Primary School, Oswestry

Lucy

L oves lillies
U nderstands others
C lever in maths competitions
Y ellow lover.

Lucy Arrowsmith (7)
Maesbury Primary School, Oswestry

Benjamin

- **B** rave
- **E** xcellent
- **N** ice
- **J** umpy
- **A** mazing
- **M** agnificent
- **I** ncredible
- **N** ew.

Benjamin Di Terlizzi (5)
St Chad's Catholic Primary School, Sedgley

Allicia

- **A** mazing
- **L** ovely
- **L** ikeable
- **I** ncredible
- **C** lever
- **I** ndependent
- **A** ctive.

Allicia Argueta (5)
St Chad's Catholic Primary School, Sedgley

My First Acrostic - The East & West Midlands

Luca Mario

L ittle
U nbelievable
C heeky
A mazing

M onkeyish
A crobatic
R avenous
I ntelligent
O bedient.

Luca Mario (6)
St Chad's Catholic Primary School, Sedgley

Summer

S weet
U nderstanding
M onkey
M arvellous
E xciting
R emarkable.

Summer Louise Davies (5)
St Chad's Catholic Primary School, Sedgley

Dominic

D aft
O bedient
M agic
I mportant
N ice
I nteresting
C lever.

Dominic Simpson (5)
St Chad's Catholic Primary School, Sedgley

Rebecca

R avishing
E xcellent
B eautiful
E xciting
C hocoholic
C razy
A ctive.

Rebecca Edwards (6)
St Chad's Catholic Primary School, Sedgley

My First Acrostic – The East & West Midlands

Isabella

I nteresting
S pecial
A mazing
B eautiful
E xcellent
L ovely
L oving
A dorable.

Isabella Everall (5)
St Chad's Catholic Primary School, Sedgley

Noah

N ice
O bedient
A ctive
H andy.

Noah Hagans (6)
St Chad's Catholic Primary School, Sedgley

Liberty

L ovely
I nteresting
B eautiful
E xcellent
R avenous
T iny
Y oung.

Liberty (5)
St Chad's Catholic Primary School, Sedgley

Siobhan

S uper
I nteresting
O bedient
B eautiful
H appy
A bsolutely amazing
N ice.

Siobhan McSweeney (6)
St Chad's Catholic Primary School, Sedgley

My First Acrostic - The East & West Midlands

Danny

D aft
A mazing
N ice
N aughty
Y oung.

Danny Joseph John (5)
St Chad's Catholic Primary School, Sedgley

Stanley

S pectacular
T idy
A mazing
N aughty
L oving
E xciting
Y oung.

Stanley Stokes (6)
St Chad's Catholic Primary School, Sedgley

Aoife

A mazing
O bedient
I nteresting
F antastic
E xcellent.

Aoife Kent-Smith (5)
St Chad's Catholic Primary School, Sedgley

Spring

S is for snails
P is for plants
R is for rabbits
I is for insects
N is for new life
G is for green grass.

Georgia Beattie (5)
St George's CE Primary School, Swadlincote

My First Acrostic - The East & West Midlands

Spring

S is for sunflowers and sun.
P is for primroses and plants.
R is for rabbits and robins.
I is for ivy and iris.
N is for new life and nests.
G is for goldfinch and grass.

Amelia Taylor (5)
St George's CE Primary School, Swadlincote

Spring

S is for sunflowers on sunny days.
P is for pigs and piglets.
R is for rain and rainbows.
I is for insects and ivy.
N is for new life and newts.
G is for greenfinches and green grass.

Ella Dingley (6)
St George's CE Primary School, Swadlincote

Spring

S is for sun.
P is for piglets.
R is for rabbits.
I is for iris.
N is for new life.
G is for grass.

Aaliyah Wall (6)
St George's CE Primary School, Swadlincote

Spring

S is for spawn and snowdrops.
P is for primroses and pansies.
R is for rain and rabbits.
I is for ivy and iris.
N is for new life and newts.
G is for goldfinch and green grass.

Joshua Fisher (6)
St George's CE Primary School, Swadlincote

My First Acrostic - The East & West Midlands

Spring

S is for sun and spring.
P is for plants and pansies.
R is for rabbits and rainbows.
I is for insects and ivy.
N is for newts, new life and nests.
G is for green leaves and green grass.

Harvey Warren (6)
St George's CE Primary School, Swadlincote

Spring

S is for sunflowers and spawn.
P is for primroses and piglets.
R is for rabbits and robins.
I is for ivy and insects.
N is for nests and newts.
G is for grass and green shoots.

Jessica Gough (6)
St George's CE Primary School, Swadlincote

Spring

- S is for sun and spring.
- P is for pigs and piglets.
- R is for rabbits and rain.
- I is for ivy and insects.
- N is for new life and nests.
- G is for green grass and leaves.

Kiera Wheatcroft (6)
St George's CE Primary School, Swadlincote

Spring

- S is for sun and snowdrops.
- P is for pigs and piglets.
- R is for rain and rainbows.
- I is for ivy and iris.
- N is for new life and nests.
- G is for goldfinch and grass.

Hannah Greenwood (5)
St George's CE Primary School, Swadlincote

My First Acrostic – The East & West Midlands

Spring

S is for springtime flowers.
P is for piglets and pigs.
R is for rabbits and robins on the bird table.
I is for ivy and insects.
N is for new life and nests.
G is for green grass and goldfinch.

Jai Evans (6)
St George's CE Primary School, Swadlincote

Spring

S is for spring and sunny days.
P is for pigs and piglets.
R is for robins and rainbows.
I is for insects and iris.
N is for nests and newts.
G is for green grass and goldfinch.

Kallum Avery-Smith (6)
St George's CE Primary School, Swadlincote

Spring

- S is for sun and sunflowers.
- P is for piglets and pigs.
- R is for rabbits and rain.
- I is for ivy and insects.
- N is for new life and nests.
- G is for green grass and green leaves.

Aimee Decamps (6)
St George's CE Primary School, Swadlincote

Spring

- S is for snowdrops and sun.
- P is for piglets and pigs.
- R is for rainbows and robins on the bird feeder.
- I is for ivy and indoors.
- N is for newts and new life.
- G is for goldfinch and greenfinch.

Emily Matkin (6)
St George's CE Primary School, Swadlincote

My First Acrostic – The East & West Midlands

Spring

S is for sun.
P is for pigs.
R is for rain.
I is for ivy.
N is for nests.
G is for grass.

Joshua Ogden (6)
St George's CE Primary School, Swadlincote

Spring

S is for sun.
P is for pigs.
R is for rabbits.
I is for iris.
N is for nests.
G is for grass.

Keegan Mulholland (5)
St George's CE Primary School, Swadlincote

Spring

S is for sun
P is for pond life
R is for rain
I is for ivy
N is for new life
G is for green grass.

Amelie Fugiel Morris (6)
St George's CE Primary School, Swadlincote

Spring

S is for sun.
P is for pigs.
R is for rabbits.
I is for iris.
N is for new life.
G is for green grass.

Natasha McInerney (6)
St George's CE Primary School, Swadlincote

My First Acrostic - The East & West Midlands

Spring

S is for snowdrops and sun.
P is for pigs and pond life.
R is for rain and rainbow.
I is for ivy and insects.
N is for newts and nest.
G is for green grass and green shoots.

Fenton Wray (6)
St George's CE Primary School, Swadlincote

Spring

S is for sun.
P is for pigs.
R is for rabbits.
I is for ivy.
N is for newts.
G is for green grass.

Maisie Simpson (6)
St George's CE Primary School, Swadlincote

Easter

E very year at Easter we celebrate the death of Jesus,
A nd the Good Friday Jesus was nailed to a Cross.
S oldiers that belonged to Judas were told to kill
the person that Judas kissed, so they did.
T he friends of Jesus were very sad that He had died.
E aster Sunday is celebrated as well because
Jesus is risen from the dead,
R emember Him from that day.

Sofia Chacón-Tuke (7)
St James' Preparatory School, Grimsby

Easter

E aster is about Jesus
A ll must pray
S ome people were Jesus' friend
T hey were happy when He was alive
E veryone was sad when He died.
R olled away the stone to the tomb.

Teddy Woodhouse (7)
St James' Preparatory School, Grimsby

My First Acrostic - The East & West Midlands

Easter

E very Easter we celebrate Jesus,
A nd we celebrate Sunday when Jesus rose from the dead,
S o Jesus came alive on Sunday,
T he Good Friday we celebrate when Jesus died on the Cross and got nailed to the Cross.
E aster is the time when we celebrate Easter.
R ude, nasty Judas said, 'The one I kiss, you imprison Him,' and Judas kissed Jesus and the soldiers took Him to prison.

Harrison Gillett (7)
St James' Preparatory School, Grimsby

Easter

E aster is when Jesus came back to life.
A ll Jesus wanted was not to die.
S oldiers took Jesus.
T hey took Jesus to the Cross.
E aster is when Jesus is very happy
R emember Him.

Amélia Lambert (7)
St James' Preparatory School, Grimsby

Easter

E aster is about Jesus
A soldier killed Jesus
S ome people did not believe in Jesus
T he people were sad
E aster is not fun for Jesus
R eal people like Easter.

Sadhbh O'Sullivan (5)
St James' Preparatory School, Grimsby

Easter

E aster is fun and exciting
A ll the disciples had bread and wine
S oldiers killed Him and put Him on the Cross
T omb is where He was put when He died
E xciting things happen and it is joyful
R isen from Earth to Heaven.

Savannah Bradley (6)
St James' Preparatory School, Grimsby

My First Acrostic - The East & West Midlands

Matthew

M arvellous
A star
T errific
T his school is
H appy
E ats
W ould like to be a hit.

Matthew Darville (6)
St Lawrence CE (VA) Primary School, Napton

Pokémon

P ikachu
O riginal characters
K ingdra
E nergy
M etamorphosis
O manyte
N asty punches.

Charlie Parsons (6)
St Lawrence CE (VA) Primary School, Napton

My Name - Sinead

S unny in summer
I ce is cold
N ice and never naughty
E njoys eating ice cream
A melia's my best friend
D oes dance class with her friend Emily.

Sinead Gillick (6)
St Lawrence CE (VA) Primary School, Napton

Chanel

C razy Chanel
H appy-hearted
A pple-red lips
N oisy music
E nergetic legs
L ittle, beautiful, blue eyes.

Chanel Oliver (5)
St Lawrence CE (VA) Primary School, Napton

My First Acrostic - The East & West Midlands

Amelia

A mazing sweet-eater
M agical as a trick maker
E njoys eating chocolate
L oves her mum and dad
I ntelligent as a teacher
A melia is my name.

Amelia Line (5)
St Lawrence CE (VA) Primary School, Napton

Jay H

J ay H loves jelly
A pple-lover
Y ummy chocolate-eater

H as a cat called Larry.

Jay Hilton (6)
St Lawrence CE (VA) Primary School, Napton

Harry Potter

H arry
A ggressive
R ich
P hilosopher's Stone
Y oung wizard

P opular person
O ld friend
T all green troll
T arantula
E normous
R eptile.

Harry Orton (6)
St Lawrence CE (VA) Primary School, Napton

John

J ohn is a jet
O n fire
H ot, hot, hot
N o more power.

John Sharlot (7)
St Lawrence CE (VA) Primary School, Napton

My First Acrostic - The East & West Midlands

Myself, Jack Field

J okey boy
A good footballer
C onfident
K ind person

F unny and fabulous
I ncredible on zip wires
E nergetic and a good reader
L ikes eating cakes
D ifferent stuff.

Jack Field (6)
St Lawrence CE (VA) Primary School, Napton

Sunny

S uper sunny sun
U nstoppable sun
N ext is spring
N ever is cold in summer
Y ou relaxing in the sun.

Catherine Bouverie-Brine (6)
St Lawrence CE (VA) Primary School, Napton

Pokémon

P erfect battle
O dd-looking creatures
K eep up, no time to lose
E nd the game with
M ighty characters
O pen a new card
N asty creatures.

Jay Ramsay (6)
St Lawrence CE (VA) Primary School, Napton

Playing

P laying Ghostbusters is great,
L ike Tia Ball.
A t playtime
Y ou can play
I n the back room.
N ow I can't play because I'm working
G oing for outside play is great.

Jack Travis (6)
Springfield House Special School, Solihull

My First Acrostic - The East & West Midlands

Family

F amily is good
A lways have fun
M y dad plays with me and Tyler
I t is nice to have my family
L ots of sisters and brothers
Y es, I love my family.

Leighton Oseman (5)
Springfield House Special School, Solihull

Dinosaur

D inosaurs have sharp teeth
I like dinosaurs
N o dinosaurs are alive in human time
O nce upon a time dinosaurs lived
S ome dinosaurs can fly
A dinosaur has scales
U nder leaves you may find dinosaur eggs
R unning dinosaurs are scary.

Beren Alesbrook-Wain (6)
Springfield House Special School, Solihull

My Dog

Max is my dog
You would like to play with Max

Dog, I love you!
Oh Max, I like to draw you
Go Max! Go!

Kieran Doyle (7)
Springfield House Special School, Solihull

Tap Dance

Taking a small step
A practise making it easy for a day
Practise, practise so much fun!

Dance, dance, I don't want to stop
And so much fun there is no stopping!
Not a chance to stop.
Can't do it, practise.
Everyone is good at tap.

Mia Bowen (6)
Tibberton First School, Droitwich

My First Acrostic – The East & West Midlands

Dangerous Dinosaurs

D inosaurs are extinct
I see electronic dinosaurs
N o dinosaur could be any colour
O nly some eat other dinosaurs
S ome are green and orange
A ll are scared of T-rex
U nless they are very small
R unning fast
S taying alive!

Torr Strange (6)
Tibberton First School, Droitwich

Footy

F ootball is fun because you score a goal!
O h now the other team scored a goal, that's very bad.
O h yes! We just scored an excellent goal!
T he goal is too small.
B ut I didn't mean to foul him!
A nd Wayne Rooney is the best man.
L osers cannot win against Man U because they are rubbish.
L osers cannot win the World Cup.

Blythe Kirkpatrick (7)
Tibberton First School, Droitwich

Worms

Worms are slimy.
Our garden is full of earth workers.
Revolting worms under everyone's feet.
Making worm castings as they slither along.
Slithering is their favourite thing.

Ross Clews (6)
Tibberton First School, Droitwich

Worms

Worms under your feet
Outside under your feet
Revolting, wriggling under my feet
Mums are scared of worms
Slimy under your feet.

Jake Clews (5)
Tibberton First School, Droitwich

My First Acrostic - The East & West Midlands

Horses

H orses are gorgeous in all shapes and sizes.
O r knows when someone's on its back.
R iding around the field is
S o much fun
E asy riding a horse
S o much fun, yeah!

Charlie Hemming (6)
Tibberton First School, Droitwich

Worms

W orms live underground
O ut in the mud
wR iggly worms
M uddy, revolting
S limy worms.

Reuben Hey (6)
Tibberton First School, Droitwich

Dancing

Design your own dance,
As you dance across the floor.
Never think that it is rubbish because it's good
Creating another and another.
Imagine you're famous!
Never think it's rubbish,
'**G**ood dancing,' said the teacher.

Georgie Lewis (6)
Tibberton First School, Droitwich

Acting

Agility is cool
Call everyone
To come and act!
It's easy to act,
Nobody is bad at acting
Good job everyone.

Ben Darby (7)
Tibberton First School, Droitwich

My First Acrostic - The East & West Midlands

Weather

Weather is always there
E very day it is sunny
A nd tomorrow it might be rainy!
T omorrow it might thunder!
H e likes weather
E veryone does
R ain tomorrow?

Harvey Newman (6)
Tibberton First School, Droitwich

Dancing

D oes everybody like me?
A nimals like me, see
N ow one animal does dance like me
C ool kangaroo does like me as well
I like myself all the time
N ow it's time I to go bed
G reat, I love dancing like animals.

Katie Vertigen (6)
Tibberton First School, Droitwich

Minibeasts

Minibeasts are kind
I squash minibeasts
Nobody wanted to play with them
I don't want anyone to stand on me
Beautiful bugs
Everybody likes me
Ants crawl around you
Some minibeasts crawl on the grass
They are flying in the air
Some minibeasts do sting you.

Maddison Johnson (6)
Whitwell Primary School, Whitwell

My First Acrostic - The East & West Midlands

Minibeasts

M inibeasts crawl up people's legs,
I t bites.
N ibbling people's legs
I t walks
B ees sting and die
E ggs hatch
A ir is cold
S ome bees sting
T hey can climb
S ome bees fly and sting.

Nathan Skinner (7)
Whitwell Primary School, Whitwell

Minibeasts

Minibeasts are amazing.

Insects can climb up trees.

Nasty stings can really hurt you.

In the sky I can see beautiful butterflies.

Bees busily collect pollen.

Enormous creatures with fantastic colours.

All the creatures love my garden.

Super, wonderful creatures have got stripes on them.

Tiny insects can go under trees.

Summer creatures love the sun.

Lewis Longden (7)
Whitwell Primary School, Whitwell

My First Acrostic - The East & West Midlands

Minibeasts

M ud is where the slimy worms live.
I nsects live in people's pretty gardens.
N ature is interesting.
I like learning about them.
B right colours fluttering across the windy sky.
E arwigs crawl under damp, dark logs.
A nts can carry heavy objects.
S top! Don't hurt the minibeasts.
T hey should live as well.
S ome people poison minibeasts! Why?

Joel Whittaker Naylor (6)
Whitwell Primary School, Whitwell

Minibeasts

Minibeasts are tiny creatures
I like the bugs
Nasty wasps who can sting
In the sun they collect their food
Busy bees with lovely stripes
Eggs in the nests
Ants running fast
Stunning flowers full of pollen
Tiny bugs too small to see
Summer is here.

Cain Womble (6)
Whitwell Primary School, Whitwell

My First Acrostic - The East & West Midlands

Minibeasts

M inibeasts can come in all shapes and sizes.
I ncredible minibeasts can fly, they have spots and stripes.
N ot many people know that bees can only sting once in their whole life.
I nvisible air is still needed for tiny little bugs.
B eautiful butterflies flutter peacefully all around.
E legant ladybirds flutter around.
A n army of ants come out to fight back the nasty humans!
S nails are so slow that you can even see them move!
T eeny tiny minibeasts crawling all around.
S piders are very, very, very scary.

Louise Machin (7)
Whitwell Primary School, Whitwell

Minibeasts

M inibeasts have amazing armoured skin.
I ncredible lashing tails.
N asty stings could kill you.
I nsects like ladybirds have beautiful black spots.
B ees have beady eyes looking for pollen.
E very minibeast scuttles in dark green grass.
A ladybird zooms past your ear in a flash.
S ome stings are poisonous.
T he minibeast should live as well.
S top trampling the minibeasts.

Lucy Forrest (7)
Whitwell Primary School, Whitwell

My First Acrostic - The East & West Midlands

Minibeasts

M illipedes scuttle around a lot.
I nsects are tiny, huge.
N asty, angry bees.
I nsects can be fast or slow.
B eautiful ladybirds have sparkling spots.
E vil bees and wasps can sting you.
A beautiful butterfly flutters.
T iny ladybirds crawl on your hand.
S piders can crawl on your leg.

Abbie Shiwell (7)
Whitwell Primary School, Whitwell

Minibeasts

M inibeasts come in different sizes.
I nsects like fuzzy, buzzy bees and bright wasps can sting.
N ectar helps make honey.
I think everything is bigger than them.
B ees make tasty honey.
E very minibeast is tiny,
A bee's job is to collect pollen from colourful flowers.
S piders are really scary and make webs that are sticky to live on.
T iny ones are the slowest.
S ome can fly high.

Dylan Ryles
Whitwell Primary School, Whitwell

Minibeasts

M inibeasts are miniscule.
I think some of these can even sting.
N ot many bugs can sting.
I think some minibeasts can fly and some cannot fly.
B ees are tiny and they can sting you.
E vil wasps like to sting you.
A mazing creatures.
S nails and slugs leave silver trails.
T errific topic.
S o much to learn.

Jaydan Plummer (6)
Whitwell Primary School, Whitwell

Minibeasts

M illipedes are always scuttling around on the hard, dirty floors.
I nsects come in all different sizes, teeny and vast.
N ectar is collected by the buzzy, stripy bee from the beautiful flowers.
I nsects aren't so scary, so you don't have to step
   on them with your massive shoes.
B ees are always buzzing around.
E arwigs have sharp pincers to bite.
A nts are always marching around.
S nails are terribly slow.
T eeny, tiny insects scampering in the long grass of the garden.
S piders are hairy and scary though.

Harvey Baker (6)
Whitwell Primary School, Whitwell

My First Acrostic - **The East & West Midlands**

Minibeasts

M inibeasts scuttling on the ground.
I love minibeasts because they have beautiful colours.
N ever ever touch a huge stinging insect.
I would never hurt an insect.
B ig caterpillars chomp through the green cactus leaves.
E ggs from minibeasts come in all colours.
A super fluffy wasp stings a human.
S nakes eat minibeasts.
T wo huge wasps buzz to find their food.
S mall bugs creeping through the ground.

Harvey Spencer (6)
Whitwell Primary School, Whitwell

Minibeasts

M ini creatures are great.
I nsects live in nature.
N ectar is collected by buzzy bees from lovely flowers.
I watch slugs and snails slide across the floor leaving their slimy trails.
B right yellow and dark black stripes means sting!
E legant butterflies flutter around.
A bee sadly dies after it stings you.
S uper armies of ants march across your garden.
T errific minibeasts.
S o interesting.

Taylor Atkinson (7)
Whitwell Primary School, Whitwell

My First Acrostic - **The East & West Midlands**

Minibeasts

M illipedes have one hundred tiny scuttling legs.
I nsects crawling everywhere in houses and schools.
N ot a sound from flies.
I ncredible colours to be found.
B ees buzz in my ears.
E very insect that you see that is a minibeast, care for it.
A nts crawling around.
S un shining down.
T arantulas crawling in people's baths.
S potty ladybirds creeping around.

Harvey Smith (6)
Whitwell Primary School, Whitwell

Minibeasts

M inibeasts can be really tiny and some can be massive.
I nstructions - the bee collects pollen from the beautiful flowers.
N o one sees minibeasts because they scutter.
I think most insects are tiny.
B rilliant bees make super honey.
E veryone knows that every creature is teeny.
A mazing ladybirds zoom through the air.
S ome creatures can sting.
T iny ants collect leaves from trees.
S ome creatures are slimy.

Mollie Godley (6)
Whitwell Primary School, Whitwell

My First Acrostic - **The East & West Midlands**

Minibeasts

M inibeasts are fluttering by.
I nsects flying in the sky.
N ot a single sound to be heard.
I ncredible colours to be seen.
B ees are collecting their precious pollen.
E ggs are being stored in a safe place.
A cocoon has been made.
S unshine in the sky shining bright.
T wo buzzing bees are working hard.
S ummer has come at last in Minibeast Town.

Lydia Allen (7)
Whitwell Primary School, Whitwell

Minibeasts

Mini worms slither through the beautiful green grass.
Insects are very smart and tricky.
Nature is where all the splendid bugs love to live.
Insects are very tiny.
Bees zoom in the wonderful blue sky.
Enormous wise bees and wasps can sting people.
Also snails are very slow and they slither on the path leaving shiny trails.
Spots of a ladybird are dark black but they how how old the creature is.
Trees are the food for some of our minibeasts.
Super creatures, I love minibeasts.

Lucy McKnight (7)
Whitwell Primary School, Whitwell

My First Acrostic - **The East & West Midlands**

Minibeasts

M inibeasts are amazing and super.
I nsects can be tiny or huge.
N o one should stand on minibeasts.
I nsects have different names.
B ees fly around the world collecting pollen from bright, beautiful flowers.
E arwigs are endangered when big feet trample around.
A nts are being trampled on!
S ome minibeasts are speedy and some are slow.
T rees are food for some of our minibeasts.
S ome minibeasts are endangered.

Caitlin Mather (7)
Whitwell Primary School, Whitwell

Arts And Crafts

C olouring is my favourite,
R eally fun!
A rt when I
F eel like it! I always
T ry really hard to make things pretty,
S ometimes I make glittery cards.

Lucy Orme (5)
Wistanstow CE Primary School, Craven Arms

Dogs

D ark
O ld
G ood
S illy dogs!

Yousef Aokal (6)
Wistanstow CE Primary School, Craven Arms

My First Acrostic - The East & West Midlands

Daddy

D addy goes to work.
A lways busy.
D ark hair with a
D og at the farm. Daddy bought a
Y oyo for me and Amelie!

Aaron Northwood (5)
Wistanstow CE Primary School, Craven Arms

Ponies

P ony is galloping
O r she is jumping
N aughty pony on the run!
Y ou are funny!

Daniel Liebrecht (6)
Wistanstow CE Primary School, Craven Arms

Strawberries

S illy strawberry
T iny strawberry
R ed strawberry
A t least strawberries are good
W et strawberry
B ig strawberry
E ating strawberries
R ipe strawberries
R eally
Y ummy strawberry!

Kaitlyn Orme (6)
Wistanstow CE Primary School, Craven Arms

Playing With Lego

L ego is fun, you can make
E verything with it.
G ood for making different things
O r putting things together.

Lewis Key (5)
Wistanstow CE Primary School, Craven Arms

My First Acrostic - The East & West Midlands

Ballet

B allet is fun
A cheener comes too!
L ong legs
L eaping
E veryone is good on
T ippy toes!

Isobel Hatton (5)
Wistanstow CE Primary School, Craven Arms

The Beach

B uckets and spades
E veryone loves it
A lways sandy
C rabs pinch at the beach
H ot beach.

Joanna Selley (7)
Wistanstow CE Primary School, Craven Arms

Ducks

D arky likes me
U p they fly
C omes home
K eeps eggs for me!

Tilly Pinches (6)
Wistanstow CE Primary School, Craven Arms

Horses

H oney horse.
O range horse
R uns down the
S treet.
E verybody loves horses.

Tegan Pinches (7)
Wistanstow CE Primary School, Craven Arms

My First Acrostic - The East & West Midlands

Cross

C rying Mary by the Cross.
R obbers by Jesus' side.
O n the Cross Jesus died.
S uddenly there was
S tillness.

Andrew Smith (6)
Wyberton Primary School, Boston

Chick

C hicks are sweet.
H ens are noisy and
I ncredible because of the
C racking eggs. I want to
K iss one, they are very sweet.

Joel Wilson (7)
Wyberton Primary School, Boston

Spring

S pring is a day to spend time with your family.
P opular flowers sitting in a garden.
R abbits run really fast and make a breeze in the air.
I like the sunshine outside in the fields.
N ow I am excited about Easter because it is here.
G ardens get really bright.

James Dawson (7)
Wyberton Primary School, Boston

Spring

S unshine is bright.
P eople love it.
R abbits jumping in the field.
I love it.
N ow it's spring.
G o and have a lovely time.

Chloe Paddison (7)
Wyberton Primary School, Boston

My First Acrostic - The East & West Midlands

Lambs

L ovely lambs laying in a field.
A little lamb jumping on the grass.
M ums and dads walking in fields.
B abies and children playing.
S pring is a nice time for lambs to be born.

Bethany Bradley (6)
Wyberton Primary School, Boston

Eggs

E aster
G loopy chocolate
G olden wrappers
S ticky mess.

Caitlin Charlesworth (7)
Wyberton Primary School, Boston

Chocolate

C racking very loudly.
H ot radiator melting it.
O to eating melted chocolate.
C hocolate gets hard in the fridge.
O to chucked hard chocolate out.
L ambs made out of chocolate.
A nimals all different sizes made out of chocolate.
T ea and chocolate cakes to eat.
E aster eggs and lots of treats.

Harry Newell (7)
Wyberton Primary School, Boston

Spring

S pring is very sunny.
P eople play outside for ages.
R abbits bounce over fields.
I n spring there's lots of flowers.
N ew flowers in spring are beautiful.
G rass grows longer in spring.

Aaron Kirkham (7)
Wyberton Primary School, Boston

My First Acrostic - The East & West Midlands

Easter

E aster is a special weekend.
A nd Easter eggs are representing the round stone.
S o when you eat an egg it will make you think of Jesus.
T hough Easter is exciting some people do not celebrate it.
E aster is a very special thing to celebrate.
R eally people love chocolate and scoff it all up.

Molly Andrew (7)
Wyberton Primary School, Boston

Bunnies

B ouncing
U p in the air
N ot near my feet
N ot on the road
I can see them everywhere,
E ating delicious grass
S itting and watching the world go by.

Henry Ellis (7)
Wyberton Primary School, Boston

Easter

Everyone together.
All eating eggs.
Special time of year.
Tasting yummy chocolate.
Eating
Roast Lamb.

Zac Baldry (6)
Wyberton Primary School, Boston

Spring

Singing birds in the trees.
Pretty butterflies in the sky.
Rabbits bouncing in the fields.
I see nature everywhere.
New chicks hatching out.
Gorgeous flowers in my garden.

Joshua Comrie (6)
Wyberton Primary School, Boston

My First Acrostic - The East & West Midlands

Spring

S unny days are here to stay.
P ouring rain can go away.
R abbits bouncing over the meadow.
I ncredible nature all around.
N ew lambs are
G razing in the fields.

Charlie Summerland (6)
Wyberton Primary School, Boston

Spring

S kipping bunnies in a field.
P eople walking in the park.
R eally cute chicks hatching out.
I see daffodils everywhere.
N ew buds starting to grow.
G rass being mowed by my dad.

Nayana Gash (7)
Wyberton Primary School, Boston

Rabbits

R abbits are bouncy
A nd rabbits have fluffy tails.
B ouncy, bouncy.
B unnies have long ears.
I can find a rabbit. Love
T o find rabbits.
S un is out for Easter.

Elliot Wilson (6)
Wyberton Primary School, Boston

Eggs

E ggs crack open
G lorious chocolate
G olden wrappers
S oon to be eaten.

Thomas Noone (7)
Wyberton Primary School, Boston

My First Acrostic - The East & West Midlands

Flowers

F lowers grow in spring.
L ight makes flowers grow at Easter.
O h no the flowers grow at Easter.
W hite flowers grow at Easter and in spring.
E aster has lots of flowers.
R oses grow in spring.
S pring has lots of flowers.

Lianne Wilkinson (6)
Wyberton Primary School, Boston

Easter

E ggs are tasty, they are nice to eat
A nd the rabbits hop around
S unflowers begin to grow
T rees grow in the spring
E aster bunnies come all around
R abbits hop all over the world.

Max Doherty (6)
Wyberton Primary School, Boston

Easter

E ggs are tasty, they are nice to eat.
A nd the rabbits hop around.
S unflowers begin to grow.
T rees growing in the spring.
E aster bunnies are bouncy and fun.
R abbits are full of joy.

Jake Smith (6)
Wyberton Primary School, Boston

Bunny

B unnies have fluffy tails.
U nusually small bunnies.
N ew bunnies sometimes grow up.
N ow spring is good for bunnies.
Y es spring is fun for us.

Tyler Robinson (5)
Wyberton Primary School, Boston

My First Acrostic - The East & West Midlands

Rabbits

R abbits are nice
A nd rabbits have tails.
B unnies are bouncy, bouncy.
B unnies have long ears.
I can find a rabbit.
T he bright
S un shines for Easter.

Madaline Pearson (5)
Wyberton Primary School, Boston

Spring

S pring is just around the corner.
P lease spring, come today.
R obins come in spring.
I love you too.
N ow all of you too.
G ood spring.

Abigail Winrow (6)
Wyberton Primary School, Boston

Bunny

B unnies have fluffy tails.
U nusual bunnies.
N ew bunnies come out in spring.
N ow spring is good for the bunnies.
Y es spring is fun for us.

Summer Houlden-Steers (5)
Wyberton Primary School, Boston

Spring

S pring is sunny.
P uppies come out.
R abbits come out too.
I n spring we have lots of fun.
N ice and cool in spring.
G et ready to go in the swimming pool.

Jamie Lawrence (6)
Wyberton Primary School, Boston

My First Acrostic - The East & West Midlands

Easter

E ggs are delicious
A nd trees are beginning to grow.
S leet goes away.
T ime goes forward in spring.
E aster is just for you.
R abbits are bouncy.

Osian Joyce (6)
Wyberton Primary School, Boston

Bunny

B unnies have fluffy tails.
U nusual bunnies.
N ow bunnies come out in spring.
N ow spring is good for the bunnies.
Y es spring is fun for us.

Cheila Vidrago
Wyberton Primary School, Boston

Easter

E ggs are chocolate
A nd trees grow
S pring is hot
T rees grow
E ggs are white and yellow
R abbits are bouncy. Some rabbits live in straw.

Ashley Strickland (6)
Wyberton Primary School, Boston

My First Acrostic - The East & West Midlands

Young Writers Information

We hope you have enjoyed reading this book - and that you will continue to enjoy it in the coming years.

If you like reading and writing poetry drop us a line, or give us a call, and we'll send you a free information pack.

Alternatively if you would like to order further copies of this book or any of our other titles, then please give us a call or log onto our website at www.youngwriters.co.uk.

Young Writers Information
Remus House
Coltsfoot Drive
Peterborough
PE2 9JX
(01733) 890066